desert noon

Desert Noon
Victoria Valentine
Lost Poetry
Copyright March 1, 2014 Victoria Valentine

ISBN-13: 978-0615982205 (Water Forest Press)
ISBN-10: 0615982204

No part of this publication may be reproduced, stored in a retrieval system or transmitted in any form or by any means, electronic, mechanical, photocopying, recording or otherwise, without the prior written permission of both the copyright owner and the publisher of this book.

Design & Layout by Victoria Valentine
Cover photo "Victoria" enriched by GinElf
ArtbyGinelf.com
Interior "Rose & Thorn" by Amanda R. Tucker

Published by Water Forest Press Books, NY
http://www.waterforestpress.com
Printed in the United States of America

desert noon

Victoria Valentine

Lost Poetry

Water Forest Press Books

Victoria Valentine

I've got my Eye on You

desert noon

For

Lady Marian
and
Gentleman Bill

His Summer Blessing
Her Winter Bliss

June & January

Together in Heaven

Amen

Contents

desert noon	10
beautiful	12
caves	14
john	16
every time you go away	18
one night stand	20
truth	22
hunting with white nails	23
crackers and gulls	24
big hat	26
quietly	28
if i were april	30
lost	31
dream #2046	32
untitled	34
untitled ii	35
in the taxi	36
she	38
west of salem	40

desert noon

dangerous strangers	41
sins and lovers	42
domino effect	44
zero to forever	46
a mind at war	48
phobia	49
words that flow	50
pink parchment	52
purgatory	54
purgatory ii	55
you and me	56
time	58
driving lessons	60
beautiful innocence	62
days of straw	64
scribblings	66
after-thoughts	68
about the author	71

Victoria Valentine

desert noon

desert coiled around me
light on my feet – movement came swiftly
champagne locks heavy, crossing my brow
shuttered an eye crystal green
with the other i squinted
denying an urge to flee home
where comfort warmed my pampered skin
not a sun brazen / relentless and sordid
as this place surrounding life without reason
thirsting i mouthed currents of air
swatting grains of sand glazing my face
raised a hand as a visor
     mindless response
         gazing sunward
from nowhere you seemed to glide
taunting endless space
tall / gilded and bold
with brandy eyes pouring smoothly
caught beneath searing skies – and one another
a prince and a drifter
distance between us mere
    as a pivot
        forcing me to the brink
barely did i raise my stare bearing down at my soles
embedded in blistering earth pale as my lips / till
my ears grasped the chords of my mind –
felt the beat of my heart

desert noon

something in the distance affirming
a faltering phrase lost in silence
closing the gap
there you stood
nearby, one man older / a woman veiled
olive-skinned / brooding
however, not as near as i who could simply reach out
swirl my fingers through charcoal madness
tufts of arrogant curls captured by linen
your jubbah swayed to a halt
briefly disturbed by a breeze
or was it my sigh?
eyes colliding / speechless
swallowed by pulse of rising heat
a knowing flashed between us in the glint of a grin
and then you were gone
fading back into that thoughtless cloud
three days sped before you sent for me
    to my thrilling surprise
        through the glare of a brilliant sun
that hammered a slice of my window shade
blinking sand from the corners of restless eyes
i knew you would never be there
in my country you'd be that heart-stopping stranger
cloaked by Armani
not caring for blonds
coarse hair bound - shading the nape of your neck
tossing a tepid glance over one shoulder
vanishing into granite, privacy glass - and steel

Victoria Valentine

beautiful

wind
always wind
rain
dancing on skylights

waves
ocean waves
silver-tipped nibbling midnight
rousing lazy stars from slumber
drizzling tinsel as they rise

music
drifting with chimes
your lips pressed to my ear
a velvet sigh

august
blazing flare
sauntering maiden
into January's world
dusted with peace

desert noon

nature knows her place

yet

things get lost in forever
poetry on a crashed drive
paradise
lovers

if you were here
i'd call this heaven

Victoria Valentine

caves

wading in Aegean currents
sun basting buttered skin
yours a Mediterranean born brown

mine yielding to tugs of the hip
your fingers and sea, as you lifted me
our legs coiling, interlocking

we'd come with the tide
then wrap in Turkish towels
exploring the caves

and each other till i felt
your damp curls in my palms
my tightening grip lingering

the morning you raised my skirt
only to lower me across a ledge
your hand stifling my moans

desert noon

so the air could not echo
when you sliced me in two
as you did the redhead

on that tour bus floor
your heaving mattress
while occupants hiked the ruins

you always owned the caves
the sea, the island you called home
the harlots you made, hesitant to leave

while the gulls soared for dinner
craning their necks apathetically
as they scooped up prey, much like you

Victoria Valentine

john

his laughter reverberated extraordinary truth
chosen words once whispered beneath
sheets of satin that hugged two figures delicately,
lighter than his uncertain trace of my skin

yet his subtle breath sighed with secrets
troubled songs, perhaps to a deafening world
of life beyond the reach of such creatures
he and i, fleeing loss beyond his gentle grasp

clover path, pebbled, guiding believers
toward a cottage in the states
where on a porch that watched a peaceful lake
he would find himself, find beauty in the world

beauty within, my dispassionate john
yearning for life's simplest pleasures
taken for granted by the unaffected
as he quietly stumbled and turned to stone

how would one wear a perfume bottle
or teddybear on a finger that longed
for a ring of promise sworn for eternity
candy and roses, bittersweet insults

desert noon

petals of flowers wrapped in rancid foil of time,
reduced to sludge inside a thoughtful box from john
compress my heart, burn to life the outline of his face,
his voice, the tips of his fingers upon my lips,
    all things fleeting
        all things good

how easy would it be to commit once again
to ashes of bridges burned, but my joyful love
failed to brace john's struggling soul
to combat mysteries of sheltered misery

did he ever believe the laughter or the whispers?
during those times of fragrant blossoms
and lash-swept tears too stubborn to surface
before he succumbed and i slipped into his past

Victoria Valentine

every time you go away
paul young

i often imagined dazzling prose
that surged and swayed with ease
like willow upon sweet wind

dreams of desire and need where
you'd fuck me in waist-deep tides
in death defying ritual

a blue tang sweeping scales from
a damsel about to spawn
barren eggs in sterile currents

your lips crushed mine but once
upon a time when we tumbled
dizzy above lavender fields

even nightmares shriek enchantment
if your lover stands before you
beckoning against the pale of the moon

desert noon

broad-mouthed corpse
you followed me racing
thru courtyards crumbling castles

only to snatch me in your arms
irresistible but fatal
raking glistening ivory about

the weakness of my flesh
emptying all that was mine
but a drop of ardent blood

my cross i pressed against your cheek
wide eyed you burned then you were gone
long before sunrise cloaked the sky

every time you go away
you take a piece of me with you
until there's nothing left behind

one night stand

you washed over me
harder than Montauk waves
on a sizzling night with no sky
me imagining those monster
swells even before I felt them

you with that irresistible dark hair
smothering my senses   quietly
my fingers knowing the curve of your mouth
yours bridging the
shivering space between us

i needed no starlight to describe
the place where i loved you
deep in my heart or was it
pounding of surf   and
your breath on my face
feeding my need
turning me on   till

desert noon

in silence we ceased
bare bottomed on damp sand
your blanket a handshake away
where scattering clothes told
a casual story
a she and anonymous he

till morning arrived
with sun in her eyes
just in the nick of time

now here i sit
scribbling a dear john
with nothing much to say
and no one to send it to
because you're nowhere around

truth

i will only love you
until one by one
each star slips from an aching sky
trailing ash across a
fading horizon

when towers crawl without shame
floods hungrily consume
desperate mountains
grinding peaks to wasteland
your name shall be the wind

when rainwashed deserts surge
plunging deeply into forests
while time seeks revenge
clocks failing to rewind

i will wreak havoc upon dusk
no longer a midnight mistress
as my sheets resolve to embers
and your face i forget
only then will i comprehend
your dying smile

desert noon

hunting with white nails

her nails are strong and white
she sips sarsaparilla from Doulton
with a curled tongue,
while a tasty breeze overrides
pacific tides
lured by a slash in window dressings,
nuzzling neat accordion tapestry
in a mansion overlooking
green cliffs
she has settled for midday tea
in his oversized drawing room.
as she licks the tip of her finger
flipping another page of the morning journal,
she reads other people's thoughts
with critical curiosity;
while a mutt in a ransacked house, downtown
circles last month's news, pacing
for a place to leave his mark upon her article
her mastiff sniffs vaulted air,
above even *her* head as
she peels back another page of print and begins
to search the want ads

crackers and gulls

sea-blanched shells, sand dollars
vacant crafts of life
strewn upon miles of winsome shore
unintentional formations
for sunrise joggers to evade,
transients to fancy

the tide burst forth narrative,
bits and pieces, trinkets of death
treasures we greedily assaulted
selecting the splendid, seeking only the flawless
we crammed leather hobos full,
destined for conformity;

the suburbs of hudson's dull existence surrendering
the lure of this day, this island, this melodrama
fantasia, foreign to ice-drizzled mountains
we'd climb our way home, soberly desert

a brilliant sunburst cresting summer's horizon
before beach-dwellers tossed tumbled stones
and the ocean revoked her remnants,
like unwanted strays dredged back to their shelter

desert noon

we pitched crackers high as small arms reach
up through salted breeze
inviting a flock of circling gulls
that swarmed our heads like agitated bees
practically brushing flat our dithering hair

ivory wings tipped with surf
they dodged and dove so close,
frighteningly daring
reminding me of you

from afar you studied a postmarked photo
where we strolled a beach crowned by dawn
two sets of footprints marring wind-brushed sands
anxious surf nibbling our knees
i loved that photo as i loved the horizon but
i loved you most

you asked several times *who'd captured that view*
wondering if we'd simply been two women alone ?
"a stranger snapped it " - i promised
your voice caught, then strained

a sleepwalker rudely awakened
should i confess he'd perched on a terrace ?
a towering vulcher amidst the gulls, the sea,
the sands, the peace, the glory, the fairy tale
the ocean between you and i

Victoria Valentine

big hat

you wore a big hat
hiding your fear
yet I noted pure beauty
framed by a hesitancy

my cares I stuffed into a satchel
tossing it far to the river
that rolled cautiously
while gulls circled anxiously

currents of turmoil
flooded calm's depth
feigning peaceful transparency
locked in uncertainty

anxious fawns flocked
amidst swaying brush dancing
between prisms of sun-day
awaiting stolen symphony

desert noon

splashes of evening's artist brush
doused visions with muted shapes of dusk
till the gulls disappeared
and the fawns slept in cover

in explosion of silence
you broke our alliance
stepped out of place
fading into midnight

you slipped on a cloud
exposing the sky
baring stars that glared down
understanding what I could not

Victoria Valentine

quietly

love me quietly
as a distant sun seeping
mutely into a vacant sea

fragile and pure as dusty snow
and starlings at dusk shyly gliding
serene as mountain streams

without fear
as trees shed leaves
upon an autumn floor

mist brushes garden's dew
mingling softly with faltering rain
drifting from an undisturbed sky

sweet bridal lace
and hush of baby's breathe
stuns fragrant heather

desert noon

and wild flowers mask
their peaceful scent
love me quietly

where gentle meadows
dissolve soberly with the
curve of the road

in the whisper of moonlight
where your silence has yet
to leave a sound

in the wake of
eternal dream
faultlessly

love me quietly
without hesitation
leaving bitterness behind

Victoria Valentine

if i were april

if I were april, apple blossoms
would utter sweetness
sprinkling peace on grassy hills like
flakes of lingering snow grasping breeze
whispering discretely, promise that

in autumn I would offer you
my hand anew, in patience
drawn from ages alone
we'd spend ourselves in amnesty
drifting on

your summer blaze
caught in fiery fields
stretching toward my winter
where you still melt jagged frost
in december pain

i remember the nights
and the moon that held secrets
of being with you
when I couldn't
if only I were april

desert noon

lost

in this room
i am alone
wondering why

the knot in this chest
stops these hands
from writing

prevents this mind from creating
weighs these feet to the floor
halts this soul's escape

staring at the phone
i cannot dial
these fingers are numb

keyboard is still
a foreign object these days
frozen, unproductive

if but one line made sense
perhaps . . . just perhaps
stubborn words would flow

the knot in this chest
tells this head to forget
but this heart is lost

dream #2046

the staircase did not wind in peace
like the spathiphyllum pathway edging
graciously toward a haven's past absorption

by the strangeness that became you and I
but instead stood steep and frightening
with decrepit railings that a delicate

hand could not grip and i felt myself
slip away each time I lunged
for that cold wrought iron wizard

that would magically transport me
to a place where you should be poised
to lift me above all this chaos

each attempt however failed hideously
to conquer the beast that swayed
alluring yet grave in a useless vacuum

desert noon

a white space abandoned and distraught
as i with each leap, there it waited
a limbless apparition with a splintered stare

leading unceremoniously, no purpose but to taunt
and hurl these disseminated arms so weak
an embrace that once held you warm and close

yet never again to cradle the weight
of an infant light and loving
no less you who will not be found

far up and away, beyond a wall of annihilation
higher than the rungs that toss a spirit in-
to empty places with no floors to fall back on

untitled

no angel caught me
while i fell to
hard stone floor
head slamming the wall
confusion and pain
for a moment i recalled
you walking away
as i lay there
i knew
should i ever rise again
it would be on my own

desert noon

untitled ii

tumbling leaves broke summer serenity
bare limbs whispered of wind alone
songbirds long gone
with them his scent
buried far too deeply was she
deeper than the unrest of his soul
shattered porcelain, fragmented beyond repair
locked in woodlands of a failing harvest

Victoria Valentine

in the taxi

i found myself
dressed in nothing
but a pink striped towel
wet hair
damp skin.

summer whispered
thru the driver's
open window;
an indian man
steering my fate
as well as a male fare's
mute silhouette

"drop me here," i muttered.
"i take the man first,"
full lips oozed
as dark eyes washed me,
the taxi gliding quickly
beyond my exit.

desert noon

a dream is a dream is a dream
ignorance is fantasy
fear surged knowledge;
he appeared
in his car, for home we sped.
"what a dream!" i recalled as
cool sheets hugged my chin.

reality wrestled nightmare
morning peace?
my satin legs draped the bed
feet crushing carpet
stumbling with sleep.
a pink striped towel!
stunned i froze . . .

"i respect your privacy
my friend, you are *not* my lover,"
i informed the mute
as the taxi stole our destiny.

salt breeze wiped my sweat
distant currents roared
one by one the houselights
each went out
a lantern rusted upon an upstairs table
i knew I'd never make it thru the darkness.

she

she's a cloud-watcher
devoted to Eeyore

kissing the sky
she signs Christ's cross
in daily scores
fingertips pressed to forehead
waiting for lightning to strike

in sparse lapse of sanity
blocking fantasy with reality
prays for vice of relief !
yet the only one she had
is stranger than she;
neither drink nor smoke
just indulge in paranoia

she left him for loneliness
and struggles with pros and cons
of celibacy
which he already decided upon

desert noon

so she listens to Bush
sing about sleeping cables
as she floats like an
embryo in a vinyl womb

a hypochondriac at heart
cursed by naivety

she couldn't tell an
asteroid from a star

or homosexual
from straight

Victoria Valentine

west of salem - jewels drown in silt

you go in and out
like the sludge-swept hudson
down that thousand meters
we call perdido en tiempo
past diamond studded lanterns
magnetic coves booked for love's semesters
chiseled by emeralds and silk worms,
grazing nothing
but
bleeding sensuous pearls
i refer to as thought
which I bury like precious rubies inside
disengaged turrets.

chaining sea-strained gates with velvet
tongue,

you go in and out
like flickering moon
thru symphonies of night fog
while you analyze holes in
the ozone layer
with meditation and gospel,
as a monk
who strums pastoral rhythm
to the beat of muffled war drums

desert noon

dangerous strangers

you showed me stars not only light the sky
how birds can fall because they fly
that the world's not only circling round
hosting life and death in every sound

air not only meant for breathing
nights not only meant for dreaming
sun not only meant for shining
words not only meant for rhyming

that a rose was born to shed its fears
in beauty on a path toward tears
and eyes can span an ocean wide
while a soul forgets to look inside

that strangers meet and have to part
soon after they have read your heart
and learned the secrets of your mind
before they leave your past to hide

that willows weep for love is blind
to those forever lost in time
and strangers of the dangerous kind
are those who leave memory behind

sins and lovers

empty as an august drought
inflicting illness upon a stream
once driven with glittering lust

dust blows in my direction
and I choke on flakes of
recollection and broken shades of truth

fortressed, yet nights hold no amnesty
my hands shake as I raise the phone
to the drone of empty echoes

and your essence sweeps my view
like a martyr in a flimsy cape
as you lunge at me

desert noon

pale faced and dull you fumble
with words that are reduced to a weak
 "i am sorry for my sin"

feeling pathetically weary
i lapse into insidious tides of repression
like simmering rays forced through

ghastly clouds that part and glide to a close
as a last curtain call with no applause
and my bow is to the death of your conscience

and the rape of my soul

Victoria Valentine

domino effect

She loves him
the other one's heart is hers
a domino effect has befallen
the planet
extending 'cross the ocean
to where my lover takes
a mistress
who rapidly beats the
waves (and me) with
her breast stroke
that vicious bitch sliced
pieces from emasculated souls!
now she wants his
he showed me the knife:
"Things will change . . .
I won't always be here for you . . ."
thank God he was blind to
the mask his bloody courtesy
plastered
across my startled face
"Kill me then, quickly,"
my desperate response,
ice crystals forming upon my

desert noon

cooling lips
now mute with knowledge
of what was to come –
or of loss
i cannot chant cognitive repertoire
when I fail to feel his pitiful song
he has succumbed so easily,
willing victim
fool that he is, my love
while helpless droplets flow
freely from invisible wounds
he proclaims weakness
yet he is strong enough
to let *me* go . . .
how can I fight what I
cannot see?
that vengeful greedy witch!
or is it just his lame excuse
shall i also succumb to her
beckoning whine?
together they drag me down
with misery's riptide
so who is the fool?

Victoria Valentine

zero to forever

a downpour raids the roof
you lie at my side
stretching your length
lying and lying and lying

morning sounds
wind breezes thru chimes
beyond the window where a
trickle of rain remains

i awaken wrapped in a cocoon
a tomb woven of cotton
in solitary confinement
lines to draw in the sand

staring at the mirror
i strain each drop of memory
while I slip thru time
no longer the willow that weeps

desert noon

throwing back my head
a voice, octaves deeper and wise
dares to be heard
i long to grow wings
take flight into darkness
relinquish humanity

i am the falcon that soars
escaping the kingdom
released from the snare
laced with danger

i am Kilauea
erupting from the core
a multitude of thousands
thirsting desert creature

i am the beast with no heart
zero to forever

Victoria Valentine

a mind at war

you come leading a flock
so I know you will not be staying.
wearing appendages
you sweep and wash and scour,

while I wake in an upstairs bedroom, alone
white silent walls meet closed doors,
glaring bruises freshly dress
sunlit parts of fleshy pallor.

yet, I am unaware of their origin.
only sorrow and tears and worry and loss
are the curiosities of mystery plundering
my troubled mind;

an arm here, a leg there, such dreams!
things in china that should
be carried upon shoulders,
not in wet ceramic bowls.

beneath the tunnel we fled.
not many emerged.
finding myself hidden under a blanket of snow,
in the cold I strained to see the two of you

had been left behind . . .

desert noon

phobia

i bathe in holy water
delivered in plastic vials thru the mail
wondering how life ever
got so empty
and what would fill your void
that has formed mine

i lie in state in my upstairs bedroom
tucked under tons of Down
and propped as high,
filled with as much misery
as that bedding that I plead to
and burrow my soul in

and hear the wane of the garage door
and the mellow mufflers of his car
and know too well the entrance chime
and the thirst of his steps on creaking carpets
and murmur "oh fuck, he's home".

he comes to me for what he calls comfort
i turn my face from his shadow to the ocean
past lives break the tempo
and I want to scream
beneath the weight that is killing me

words that flow

life's been dry for months
no rain, nothing like a thunderstorm
induction to romantic interlude

bereft my eyes won't even cry
pollen puffs fill the air
with the chorus of those birds

outside my window waking me at 5
they chatter they screech
this morning, emitting no less a quack!

but i dont live on a farm with ducks
and horses or i'd be Lady Godiva
sipping a chilly Royale

instead I'm Rapunzel
stuck up here in this castle
but beneath my window no charming paces

desert noon

tossing petals of roses savoring my name
i can't rid myself of tragedy
must have cut my hair too short

for my prince fails to reach me
or perhaps went missing in the brambles
of his sylphic dementia

still there is windsong, my child
a daughter with hair so pink skin so fair
while another lies severed within Freud

life's delicious with chocolate champagne--
thru lens of emerald lea cerulean sky
adrift beyond a fingertip, a raindrop,
a good & plenty smile

pink parchment

reaching for your outstretched hand
the sea beckoned not so far
i yielded richness of your waves
draping dark on shoulders bold
bridging curves of thirsting dunes

floating like driftwood
my knees tasted hips
tossing soundly in breakers
shattering landscape froth
sun flower at sun set . . .

knee deep in daffodils
bare toes rake sullen earth
i find my self blundering
a lea of balmy innocence
where we sampled champagne

desert noon

played ring around rain
as a sun fought with might
careless star pitching night
tore a hole in gray sky
forged a mocking black eye

whispering futility
your silence my sigh
words not exhausted
no theme for good bye
perhaps some tomorrow
my story will draw

lines on pink parchment
daring the light
the lure of the moon
the look in your eyes
your rise with the tide

Victoria Valentine

purgatory

as tangled vines of jungle weeds
he skulks, wrapping psychosis about
my flailing limbs searching,

squeezing succulent juices
from exotic fruit while
he stalls a breath

the air in my lungs stagnant
as his brain conceals
wickets of dominance and

sickness he calls devotion
while i flounder quartered and burned
as a pagan in the light of Christ

desert noon

purgatory ii

you fell back into that dark place
bitter scowl caught me by surprise
that lingering troll
fighting like hell
trapped between the poles
of your psyche
tilted
spinning like a planet
angry
no self control
spewing pain into air
stinging
you
turn me to a jack rabbit
running running faster faster
ss that my reflection in the mirror
escaping down the hall ?

Victoria Valentine

you and me

days indifferent
nights identical, bent
like a curve in a bumpy road

sleep, unrequited love
restless luxuries
neither can be found
within a cold turkey

small talk flanks bland space
modest and bare
echoes falter with
less than nothing left to say

tree limb trapeze
fell with the storm
fertilizing fields where
we once grew from seedlings

desert noon

caught in winter snow
we withered and angered
dissolved beneath footsteps
seeking amicable exile

letters stopped coming
phone line coiled in anguish
shocked by reality
passed out on the floor

then the doorbell rang
as the wind heaved a sigh
i called out in my loudest voice
but you weren't there

Victoria Valentine

time
for frank & fanny

overstuffed bronx bungalo
cropped stucco on peek-a-boo slab
grief stricken after
new owners burned her to the ground
hot irons and frilly curtains
don't do well unattended
grandpa washed that little house green every spring
beating apple buds to the punch
he'd drink a cold one
hum september song to grandma
while she baked peach dumplings
i'd climb the highest branch
brooding in my adolescent cradle
smoking fake cigarettes, popping m&m's
from a medicine bottle hoping they'd
make me grow faster
so i could look like red-mouthed models
in cosmetic commercials
with long painted fingernails
no acrylics no silicone
people were real those days
some unforgettable like

desert noon

the old goat lady staring down at me quizically
from her next door tower, scowling
she'd pose in a grimy window
stalker by day, sentinel by night
hollow-faced counting her goats pass by
that old cherry tree border – king kong tall
defending the yard
from spooky intruders that might have invaded
our creaky old shed while *we* slept like the dead
i know now something else shadowed the
old woman's face
fear of being snatched by the reaper if she
sneezed a breath
or closed an eyelid a moment too long
time is like the briefest breeze
tossing blossoms onto earth
their time of beauty spent and worthless
sprinkling feebly crocus'd dirt
they reconstructed ashy ruins
brand new from top to bottom
still that trusted slab remembers
even flames can't demolish memories

driving lessons

the platters crooned their magic touch
thru chevy bellaire speakers
i learned to drive on lonely roads
you claimed would be much easier

we straddled leather side by side
your hand atop mine reaching
while fingers roamed around my thighs
you were such a damn good teacher

in sister's room one night upstaris
right after sunday dinner
you wrapped me in your arms so close
crushing youth against your firmness

my body didn't know that burst
of heat it felt inside
only that it wanted more
of what i wasn't sure

desert noon

when you nibbled at my sister's mouth
so late one friday night
i was certain it was envy
as i hid behind the gate

when you crept up from behind
and clutched her by her breasts
i couldn't figure why she winced
or the flush that flawed your face

when you tried it with my mom though
did you really think you'd score?
i'd never seen such wrath
as when she threw you out the door

i tossed away dear diary
sweet innocence reprieve
you were such a bad boy
and i was so naive

Beautiful Innocence

The asphalt seethed with August heat as the young women made their way up a rickety iron staircase to lie aloft in protective calm. The catwalk of the abandoned lighthouse was perfection, overlooking the quiet sea licking its cove in noon blaze.

Sunshine grasped the brilliance of the brunette's flowing waves, while the other's amber tresses stroked her lovely face with flaming streaks of rainbow hues.

Wearing broad sunglasses, toting bags of lotions, music and bottled water, they found their place, positioning themselves comfortably upon a pair of wind-beaten chaise lounges.

Unleashing the ties of their halters, a soft flow of cotton drifted rhythmically to settle upon the harsh surface beneath their bare feet.

"Pass me your lotion, will you?" one murmured, a hand over her brow, her shield against a glaring swath through lacy clouds. "This is a great day . . . but we can burn." Slipping from her denim shorts, she proceeded to lavish her graceful limbs and torso indulgently, smoothing to a shimmering bronze.

desert noon

"Don't forget to cover your head," she warned. "We have to ensure our future beauty." Carefully she made certain the small terry face cloth shaded her features from any intrusive rays.

Her girlfriend giggled as she pulled a thirsty white towel from the bag, also assuring her assets would remain aglow with dew of youth. "So we can lure and keep our millionaire husbands in line . . . forever gorgeous and rich."

Toasting front to back rotisserie style, an hour elapsed. "Goodness, there's a lot of air traffic today," one remarked innocently. "Just like when we tried to do this at the marina . . . We're alone, then suddenly the place is a mob scene of cruisers."

"Of course," the other laughed. "We're in Maine this month, silly. Not Spain . . ."

"Well — we certainly seem to bring out the tourists . . ." she appeared perplexed.

Days of Straw

Remember when we did that moonless all-nighter at the Catskills? The glare of my headlights the only way we judged the immensity of that deserted barn we crashedin (not into.) The biting nostril filling-odor of dank straw mixed with damp earth, still lingers in the atmosphere around me from time to time.

Inside that pitch black sanctuary of decaying wood, stale air and mounds of haystack beds, you cradled me in your arms to keep me safe from the insanity surrounding us (our inebriated friends.)

I can still feel the tickle of your wavy dark hair brush my cheek, as your gentle arms hugged me protectively like a brother with his little sis. I would have liked more, but I never told you.

Although we had no idea of how we discovered that place at midnight, we managed to find our way home first ray of dawn — breaking the sound barrier into town, along with noon sun.

How many mornings did we drink ourselves sober? I would sleep for a few hours — then squint awake to the happy sound of Buds popping and laughter.

desert noon

An acquaintance said she saw you last week on Park, and confided you look great. I guess these days, along with friendship we'd share matching handbags.

Remember my big old boat of a black Pontiac convertible with that gorgeous burgundy leather interior? A beautiful warrior marred only by a hole in the floorboard we used as a disposal — litterbugs that we were — these days we would end up with a fine—or drinking and driving (you with your weed) would land us in the slammer. We lucked out — so did our world!

My mom complained all we shared together was a cigarette, she and I. Your mom whispered secretly to me that the lucky girl to marry one of *her boys* would inherit her beautiful suburban home. In retrospect, it was tempting, bringing to mind the telepathy I possessed, as well as the intense attraction for your older brother — always sensing when he'd
blow into town.

We lived for each other back then, all for one, wild and free. Now the highlight of my life is sprawling naked on my country deck in the summer sun —
wishing the heat on my bare skin was
your brother's hands.

Victoria Valentine

scribblings

pink nosed kitten peeks
through bushes of roses red
shy my lover's blush

if not for his face
winter would cover my heart
forever frozen

icy raindrops fall
rudely tapping budding trees
dying without him

dampening sunrise
promises of cold raindrops
my soul fights darkness

campfire flames beach
dusk ocean waves competing
signaling souls home

beacon shouts harshly
we scramble toward a lighthouse
calming our shoreline

desert noon

frolicking icecaps
swarm in warm ocean tides still
refusing to melt

intimate sonnets
the poet mends broken hearts
forgiving all sins

intimate strangers
lovers lifting fallen souls
together again

feeling as if i've
been through a war
loving you has taken
its toll
a most beautiful
injury
from which i hope
i never heal

Victoria Valentine

afterthoughts

news and undertow

read the story of the woman who loved the man,
on the front cover of the daily news
before they went under
how she scrawled across that page with thought;
if there are to be seasons
changes must take place

confusion

he's over there, finding himself, while she sits here
"not waiting" for him to make up his mind about
the philosophy of life. in ancient times, they would
have done this in fresh air, beside pillars and flowing
waters. he does it in front of the television set,
behind closed doors. She created a monster he is
slowly destroying. her love.

desert noon

scones

"Oh God," she sighed quietly to the empty room.
opening the box of scones he had left for her early
that morning, she realized who she was. her lover
was abroad, becoming a distant memory. although
this one was not handsome or exciting, he was
steady — and after all, he had thought of her at 5 am.

best

"send your very best!" they had advised.
there she sat, for hours,
concentrating above alternative blare – okay now . . .
my very best —
what would that be? (tongue click) let me think . . .
how would you "define" best?
she had never inhaled this predicament before . . .
she turned the music off for better concentration –
and with it went her confidence.

Victoria Valentine

possession

the sixties seep thru my pores
gurgling crude from a virgin well
black sludge staining tides like minds
decades of penance
that shuttle to DC
where we carved out an angel
i made my confession long ago
still can't pull the grief from my soul

collections

let them wait in line
while my bones turn to dust
spirit for life has
left this body
riddled with thorns like
colletia paradoxa
facing extinction
with my own cross to bear

desert noon

About the Author

Victoria Valentine, author and indie book publisher, resides in New York. She has been published online and in print magazines in the USA, UK, France, India, and in South Africa. She writes romance and thriller novels as January Valentine and erotic stories as Lana Lundon.

continued

Victoria Valentine

Victoria enjoys hosting her radio show, *Away With Words*, every Wednesday @ 6:30 pm EST on blogtalkradio.com, where she interviews writers and poets.

Her books include:
Wheel Wolf (Bestselling werewolf horror paranormal)
Sweet Dreams in the Mind of a Serial Killer
Fighting For You new adult romance
Beautiful Experiment, Book One, Island of Defiance Trilogy teen fantasy romance
Love Dreams contemporary romance
The Cutest Little Duckie color storybook
Desert Noon romance poetry collection
Newly Bred With Magic erotic fantasy
Seven Day Wonder, erotic fantasy written as Lana Lundon
Snowed In Anthology (erotic stories by five authors)

desert noon

Victoria is currently working on a sequel to *Fighting For You*, which is told from Indigo's point of view. Watch for *Running From Regret* in 2014.

Find January Valentine & Victoria Valentine on Amazon.com, Barnes & Noble, Kobo, iTunes, and Water Forest Press Books.
JanuaryValentine.com
VictoriaValentine.net
WaterForestPressBooks.com
http://waterforestpress.miiduu.com (Bookstore)
http://www.blogtalkradio.com/aww1 (Away With Words)
http://januaryvalentine.blogspot.com/ (Blog)
http://victoriaskyline.blogspot.com/ (Blog)
http://waterforestpressbooks.com/VictoriaValentineMailingList.htm

www.ingramcontent.com/pod-product-compliance
Lightning Source LLC
Chambersburg PA
CBHW032121040426
42449CB00005B/559